T0065565

I Was a Child but Not

Deanna Jones

authorHOUSE®

AuthorHouse™ UK
1663 Liberty Drive
Bloomington, IN 47403 USA
www.authorhouse.co.uk
Phone: 0800.197.4150

Published by AuthorHouse 08/04/2016

ISBN: 978-1-5246-2312-8 (sc)
ISBN: 978-1-5246-2311-1 (e)

Library of Congress Control Number: 2016912638

Print information available on the last page.

Dedication

To my dear husband, Michael,
who left this world, and entered
into the next. He took a part of
me with him.

Contents

Chapter 1

Life at home

It is 3:30 in the morning as I am sitting by the window. Sleep had eluded me again. Quietly watching the snowflakes falling, I am preoccupied with thoughts of my dear husband, Michael, who had passed away over a year ago. After almost twenty-five years of marriage, our beautiful daughter, Alexis, has now become my primary focus.

Compassionate people have told me that it is going to get easier as time goes on. How do they know? They are not me. The pain and hurt are just as real tonight as the day God called Michael to his heavenly Home. At times I am very angry with God for taking Michael. I know that he is in a better place but that does not help my feelings. I know that when it is my turn to leave this earth, I will be with him again.

As I sit here in contemplation of my future, the past suddenly sweeps over me. It seems like such a long time ago since I was a little girl in a family of seven: mom, dad, two brothers, and me, along with two sisters. Within the past several years I have lost my dad, younger sister, mom and older brother. The pain of my childhood is coming back to me.

When you are a child, you should feel safe, but that was not my experience. I recall from a very early age the abuse and anger expressed by my parents in aggressive ways.

One day I was looking in the baby carriage where my sister was lying. I was four years older than her. Dad walked over and told me to stay away from the baby. Then he pushed me so hard that I hit my head against the wall. He looked at me in anger. I always considered that since this incident he did not like me.

Dad was so hard on most of us when we were growing up. Three of us, my older brother Paul, my sister Susan, and I were beaten and abused whenever he felt that we deserved it. The other two were punished as well, but not as severely. He usually demonstrated some affection towards them.

On reflection, Dad had experienced a rough childhood though his mother loved him and his sister who was six years older. She was their dad's favourite and could get away with anything.

From what I was told she was a beautiful Christian lady. He never forgot how she died in his arms when he was eighteen years of age. She had suffered from stomach cancer at only forty-eight years of age. I regret never to have met my grandmother.

My grandfather remarried three more times and was killed, along with a woman he had with him, when he hit a truck on a highway.

Contrary to my wishes, I was forced to go to the funeral home to see Grandpa. I did not want to view a dead body but was given no choice.

I was crying when my aunt and cousin took me up to the casket. While there I witnessed my step grandmother removing the ring and watch from my grandfather's body. Dad was very angry over my

emotional reactions during the wake and did not want me to be at the funeral. That was a relief!

Having survived two wars, World War 11 and the Korean War, Dad came home displaying symptoms of Post Traumatic Stress Disorder. He became abusive from excessive alcohol consumption, had nightmares, and was emotionally unstable. Dad had been a sniper in the army and during World War 11 was devastated when his friend was blown up in front of him.

My mother's family differed from Dad's background. Her mother had herself suffered through a difficult childhood, and was known to be the boss. She was not kind to my mother. In fact, Grandma was unusually hard on Mom. Though her younger siblings could do no wrong, my mother bore the brunt of Grandma's anger. I am thankful to know them today as my very kind aunt and uncle.

I heard about the occasion when Mom was helping Grandma with her canning. They were making jam.

Grandma was using one of those huge, old, heavy canning kettles which had been given to her by my great grandmother.

The water in the kettle was boiling when Grandma told Mom, who was around ten years old, to take the kettle off the stove. The task was too difficult, and as Mom tried to lift that kettle which was extremely heavy for her, the boiling water poured all over her.

Mom screamed incessantly from the burns that covered her body. What the hell was my grandmother thinking? She knew damn well that my mother was just a child and could not lift that kettle off the stove.

I always felt that it was deliberate.

Grandma was also very mean to Mom at Christmas and at other events. While her siblings received more expensive gifts and treats, Mom's presents and clothes were cheaper. While the other two were treated with respect and looked up to, Mom felt extremely unloved.

Mom had a pet dog, a German shepherd. One day when she was with her family at the Lutheran church for her first communion, the dog got off the leash, ran onto the road and was killed. Mom sobbed when she returned to this scene. Grandma, on the other hand, thought it was humorous, and laughed.

How could she? As parents, we are to love our children and to keep them safe. Many parents with their own problems play favourites and seem unable to provide love.

I was not among those of my grandmother's favourites. However, I recall my grandfather being a quiet, kind, business man, but doing what he was told. He often sat with a cigar in his mouth, laughing at cartoons he watched on TV. My siblings and I liked to play with his hair, combing it and getting a dime or quarter for our attention. I was sad when he died.

My Grandma's family were known for their involvement in the occult. They practiced fortune telling, witchcraft, reading tea leaves, performing séances, pronouncing curses, and playing with the Ouija board. I recall how they propped the broom upside-down to keep the demons out.

Mom continued these practices as she grew up. She was known as a white witch who could do good and bad and was adept at discerning individuals when telling their fortunes. When she herself went to a fortune teller, she was told that she was capable of reading her own fortunes. The same mysterious things happened in my home as at Grandma's house. When I left my parents' home to get married, I denounced practices of the occult and their effects on me.

Mom and Dad were engaged when it was time for him to go to war. Mom stayed with her parents where she continued to live with the challenges that had been part of her childhood. She had endured bullying, along with the physical and emotional abuse by her mother when her sister died at birth. Mom's position changed to that of the oldest sibling. When she married Dad, she was insecure, shy and fearful.

Dad had sent money home for Mom to put away for their wedding and the anticipation of buying a house.

Her parents borrowed that money, saying that they would return it, but that did not happen.

Dad sustained a gunshot wound and was transferred for medical attention to England where his father's family lived. While there he met a woman with whom he fell in love. I have always wondered if he left a child behind in England.

He felt that because he had already committed himself to Mom, he should go home, tell her, and get some of his money back. What a surprise to find that it was all gone! I wonder if he came home for the money or for the sense of commitment that he may have felt towards my mother.

He proceeded with his initial plans to marry my mother though I do not know how he felt about this. Mom and Dad were both very unhappy people. I am aware of so many negative factors in their developing years that were not conducive to the development of a strong relationship.

Dad exercised total control over Mom and our family, and he communicated that to all of us in no uncertain terms.

Dad's childhood friend, Fred, was often around, especially on weekends. Dad and Fred had lived next door to each other when they were young boys. They had done everything together.

Fred was scary, heavily into drinking, gay, but also a pedophile. He took a liking to young boys and girls. I was just four years of age when I began to encounter horrendous problems with him. He told me that I looked pretty and he wanted to see the colour of my panties. Then he pulled them down and smelled my bottom. Fred told me to keep this a secret between the two of us, but I related this incident to my mother who in turn told Dad.

My parents sat me down at the kitchen table and I told them again what Fred had done. Dad responded with anger towards me. I did not understand why I was treated this way by either Dad or by Fred.

Fred's abuse of me repeated itself over and over. I dreaded every weekend when he would be at our house. When I looked for help from my parents, Dad's anger increased to the point where I became very frightened of him. He started showing his hatred towards me.

From the ages of four to thirteen the sexual abuse increased from bad to worse. Fred started feeling me up, licked my bottom, and also put his penis into my vagina, as well as attempting to get into my backside. He also forced me to perform oral sex which he called a blow job. I had no understanding of what this meant at that time.

I was just a little girl and didn't know where to go for help. Every weekend Fred returned for another dose of personal pleasure at my expense. Though my parents turned their backs on my predicament, they were still my parents and I didn't want anyone to take me and my siblings away. I yearned to be a normal little girl.

At the age of seven we lived in an area where my siblings and I walked just two blocks to get to school. There were a few weeks when I was an hour late for school every day. I had discovered a pretty bush with flowers nearby and in this safe setting, little animals kept my interest. In these surroundings I pretended that I was someone who lived elsewhere. I was a little girl, going into my own safe world.

The school finally contacted my parents and wondered what was happening to me. My parents were very angry with me and told me that if it happened again I would be in serious trouble. My behaviour became strange even at home. My mind was in turmoil as I wondered if these were actually my parents, and thinking that they would not treat me like this. I also questioned if these were my siblings. I moved deeper into my own little world.

My behaviour became irrational. I started running around the kitchen table, counting and looking for my real parents, brothers and sisters. I thought they were wearing masks, disguising who they really were. Then I ran back the same way, counting the people I had left. I was fantasizing and was gripped by fear. I wanted only to feel safe.

Mom began to get nervous over my actions. She said that if I did not stop acting like this, she was going to get help for me. To this day I wish she had followed through on this.

I had no social life. Being quiet and insecure, I was considered to be different from my peers.

I became self-conscious of my appearance. Mom insisted that I wear long dresses. After I left the house, I pulled the hem up above the knee. Still, I was looked on as a weird-o. During my childhood I was invited to only one birthday party on the condition that I buy the girl a large gift.

We moved again and I had to settle into another public school. Relocating twice in a short while was difficult.

At this time I was eight years old and the school nurse arrived at our home to see my parents. The school had considered placing me into the special needs class because I was having difficulty with focusing. I just sat in a trance, consumed in thought and filled with fear from the repeated abuse I was experiencing at home. This scared Dad into telling Fred that he had to leave for a while until he changed, and could keep his hands off of us.

However, Dad continued to visit Fred; going instead to his house for visits. Eventually Dad let Fred return to our house while I was developing deep fear of both men. Dad's hate for me was growing so I decided not to go for help to either parent again.

Fred often cornered me, following me to my room when no one was watching. Whenever he could get privacy with me he used the opportunity. He also started giving me dimes and quarters as a treat so that I would keep silent. In later years thoughts of these coins made me feel cheap inside. In my mind there was nothing I could do but endure what was happening to me. The sexual actions continued to get worse. There was no letup when Fred was in the house. I had no recourse.

It happened one weekend when I was nine or ten years old, while Mom had to work, that Dad's friends, Bryan and Fred were in the house. When they ran out of beer Dad left to buy more.

I went to my room where I found Fred. He was intoxicated and he wanted me. I remember how he laid me on the bed and took my clothes off. Then he put his penis into my vagina as he came on top of me. I still did not know what this was all about. He then wanted me to lick his penis in his desperation for oral sex. He stayed in my room a while longer and returned downstairs just before Dad got home.

The following day after school, when I was playing with my sisters, Dad saw me and told me angrily to go to my room and that he would be up to see me. He had told Mom about Bryan having mentioned to him that Fred and I were upstairs for a while, doing whatever while he was out getting beer. Dad was embarrassed and cornered, which he always tried to avoid, so he had to find a way out of this mess.

So Dad took it out on me. Instead of going to the man who along with himself was destroying me, I got the full brunt of Dad's wrath. He took his leather belt, and told me to pull down my pants. I was allowed to keep only my panties on. Dad then hit me thirty-five times. I counted as the hits kept coming. My backside and legs were full of welts and the force broke some of my skin. I bled a bit. However, I did not cry. There was so much anger, pain, and hurt inside of me that was turning to hatred.

Dad said that I could not have supper so when Mom came into the bedroom, I asked for permission to have at least a piece of bread but she refused to grant my request. She told me that I was being punished, to which I responded, "For what?" Mom said that it was for my behaviour the other day.

"I didn't do anything wrong. It wasn't my fault. It was Fred. Why am I being punished?" I questioned. At that time Mom did as she was told.

The following day after school, Ray, the boarder in his sixties who lived with us for two years, came to me and said: "I didn't know that you were that kind of a girl." Ray had overheard what was happening and asked Dad about it. Dad told him that I was a bad girl, that there was something going on between Fred and me, and that I was in the wrong. I did not understand until I was older.

How could Dad be so cruel? He made me look so bad though I was just a child. Dad was blaming me for his friend's actions. His buddy could do no wrong; it was all his daughter's fault.

I began wetting the bed, had nightmares, and just wished that I could die. In fact, I prayed that God would let me die. I felt like there was nothing left to live for and no one to turn to for help.

One night, at a time when my sisters and I shared a room, my older brother, being still awake, saw Fred enter our room. He got up and noticed Fred under the bed. Paul quickly went to our parent's room and related this to Mom who was still awake. When Mom awakened Dad, he said angrily, "Never mind. Go back to sleep."

As Paul told me about this the next day I realized that these were the people responsible for providing care and protection for me. I heard it again: they didn't care.

I was bullied and shunned at school. The only way anyone would play with me there was if I paid them a dime or a quarter. So at times I did.

My siblings did not understand me at all. I was considered to be different and they picked on me for that. The root of my problems was in my home where I did not feel of worth or wanted. There were so many situations, so much pain and grief.

During this time of life, I recall Dad putting a duck into the basement. My siblings and I grew fond of this new pet and paid no attention to what Dad's plan might be. After two weeks Dad killed the duck for dinner. When forced to eat it, I gagged. It was another upsetting incident for me.

One evening when getting ready for bed, I went downstairs for a glass of water. Dad had been drinking and he wanted me to sit on his lap. When I refused he insisted. This scared me. He felt me up, and went under my top and bottoms. After he finished he told me to go to bed. I lay awake most of the night, scared and angry that Dad would do such a terrible thing to me.

I kept this to myself until I left home to get married at nearly nineteen years of age. I then told Mom who had a talk with Dad but of course he denied it. He was good at lying. By this time I had lost all respect for

Mom. She could never support me. No matter what Dad did to me, she stood by him at all cost. However, I still loved her; she was my mother.

I was in my preteen years when Dad let his friends move in with us after their house burned down. This couple, Joe and Jane, had three boys, ages 15, 13, and 10.

The year they spent with us was extremely miserable for me. The two older boys were interested in me sexually. They attempted to rape me at various times.

I did not tell my parents. Why bother when Joe and Jane were heavy drinkers like my dad. The police came to our house often during the time that they lived with us. The boys got themselves into all kinds of trouble: stealing, drinking, and getting into many fights.

It was a relief when they moved into their own home. After Joe and Jane separated, he got depressed, got drunk, and ended up in jail. While there, Joe hung himself and died.

My parents did not associate with Jane and her family after this happened. However, Fred was still my constant concern.

His last evil molestation occurred when I was thirteen, sleeping in the same room as my sisters. I shared a bed with Susan. Fred, as usual, had stayed overnight and was drunk. I awakened from sleep with a start when I felt someone touch me. Fred was performing things on me that he should not be doing. I tried to wake up Susan but he told me to be quiet. He had a wild look in his eyes. I was so scared that he would hurt me; I decided to keep my mouth shut. Then he left the room.

The next morning I told Mom with determination that Fred was going to stop or I would go for help. Mom said that she would talk to Dad. I told her, "Okay, but it is going to stop NOW!"

Dad intervened in his own way and told Fred to stay away. However, Dad visited Fred often at his place. He couldn't stay away from him.

Life in my teen years just got more difficult. My parents lied about me and it became apparent that these falsehoods became reality to them. I continued to experience their hatred and abuse.

When I started high school, my low marks in public school destined me for the Opportunity Class. The students did not like me as I was considered to be so different from them.

One day I was invited to a party. It was a good thing that I did not go. I heard the next day at school about the plan to get me drunk and to rape me.

I stayed at that school for only one year. It was too much for me emotionally as I had again experienced rejection and bullying.

Dad was a very troubled man. There were numerous occasions when he took some or all of us in the car with him. He usually parked at a hotel. In spite of Dad's promise that he would be only a few minutes, no matter what the weather, there were times when we sat in the car for a few hours. Dad was in the bar getting drunk or fighting with someone. He forgot that we were outside waiting for him.

I still felt sorry for Mom. Her life with Dad was hard. At times he treated her like garbage. Mom, in turn, would then take it out on the five of us, especially if our behaviour became annoying to her. With her hands or whatever she could find, she beat us.

Sometimes we got away from her and hid under the bed. Not letting that stop her, she dragged us out by the hair and continued beating us. She certainly lost control of herself.

Altercations between Mom and my older brother were increasing. Due to our home life, Paul had severe emotional problems. One day Mom chased him through the house holding a butcher knife. They ran out through the front door and around the house. Our neighbour across the street was watering her flowers, looked up as she heard the commotion, and had the look of horror on her face. Yet Paul maintained a love for Mom no matter what he went through.

Since Paul and I were the two oldest siblings, we interacted together more than with our younger siblings. One day he wanted me to run away with him but I refused because I did not want to get into more trouble. So he ran off on his own. By walking and hitchhiking he got many miles away from home, eventually getting to our grandparent's barn. He was found there several hours later, after my anxious parents searched for him and contacted family. This infuriated Mom and Dad. I was so sure that if I had been with Paul in this venture, I would have been the recipient of a severe beating.

When I entered Business School, I began to experience some success. I then began working and my parents, thinking that they needed the money, took my income. I wonder if this is all they thought I was good for.

My first job was in the office of a mail room. I soon discovered that some of the male employees thought they had the liberty to lay their hands on me by putting their arms around me and making suggestive gestures. They also used foul language. I could not focus on my workload as I experienced flashbacks of my childhood. I decided to quit my job.

Since my parents had become used to getting my money, Mom, who anticipated that Dad would react negatively, became extremely upset over the job loss. To show it, she raised her fist in a rage of anger. I immediately walked away from her and hid in a closet but she forced the door open and continued to beat me.

My siblings all experienced their own problems related to our home life. I was not close to my younger brother or my sisters.

I remember when my brother Paul was almost eight years old, and I was six, we had a little friend who lived near us. Her name was Marie and she played with us frequently.

We lived near a lake with a lot of water snakes for a while. During that time our friend drowned after falling into the water. She had ignored instructions to stay away from the water. Help had arrived too late.

Marie's mother was beside herself with grief and could not go to the funeral. The hearse was driven past our house and my brother and I waved goodbye. Then it travelled on to the house of Marie's family.

As I think about my oldest brother, Paul, my memory goes back to his teen years following his hospitalization for advanced rheumatic fever.

He began to get into a lot of trouble.

At the age of fifteen, he and his friend stole cigarettes and started a fire in front of the police station.

Through the use of a pay phone these boys made calls that sent a hearse to a house, ambulances to various homes, sent police cars on a chase, ordered restaurant deliveries like Pizza Hut to be made for unsuspecting people.

Police were searching all over for whoever was placing these calls but could not find the perpetrator.

The newspaper carried a report of these shenanigans but it was only later that Paul admitted his actions to our parents.

Not long after, Paul was admitted to the psychiatric ward of the hospital due to a mental break-down. He remained there for a lengthy period of time and was on many kinds of medication.

Paul went through a time when he was in and out of hospitals, including mental institutions. On one occasion he broke a nurse's arm and was placed in a padded cell.

After he got married, Paul and his wife, together with her family, drank a lot. She and her family mistreated Paul. One night when he was drunk and went to bed, his two brothers-in-law put a long snake into his bed. The next morning the snake was still there. Paul nearly went crazy.

His wife and her two brothers thought it was a big joke. I reacted to it with disgust.

Paul and his wife had one child, Dean, who was growing up to become a fine young man. At twenty-one years of age he was killed in a truck accident.

Paul, who by now was divorced, went through deep grief in the loss of his son. It almost destroyed him as he turned to drinking even more and experienced deep depression.

You never get over the loss of loved ones. You either live with it or it destroys you.

After Paul's wife, Jean, left him he lived in a boarding house. There was also a lengthy time when he lived on the streets, often sleeping in parks because he had no place to go.

In spite of what Paul endured or how he was treated, he expressed a lot of love and forgiveness. However, his body reacted to all the drugs he had been on and he suffered from a stroke. His personality changed as a result.

I remember Paul going to the country with Dad and Mom where they stayed with people who owned a motel. When my parents left, Paul stayed behind for another two weeks. He drank the entire time he was there.

When he fell asleep with a cigarette in his hand, it fell into the mattress and started a fire. As a result two motel units burned down. Neither the owners nor the police laid charges as he had not done this intentionally. Miraculously Paul did not lose his life in the fire.

In later years Paul moved in with Mom and cared for her after Dad's death. After Mom died, Paul came to live with us. This lasted for only eighteen months before he died of a blood clot to his lungs.

Paul and I had established a close relationship and his death was very difficult to accept. It happened so quickly. It seemed like he was here, and then he was gone. I still miss him very much.

When my youngest sister, Jennifer, was very small, Mom went through a time of severe illness and could not care for all of us. She spent a long

time in the hospital and was confined to bed. Jennifer, being the baby of the family, went to live with our grandmother during this time. The rest of us had various babysitters until Mom's health had improved.

Dad was not handling the situation well. He had difficulty dealing with the responsibility mom's inability laid on him.

Jennifer became very close to Grandma and wanted to stay with her. Then when Mom went to bring her home, Grandma didn't want to let her go. Mom said, "She's my child, not yours." With that she took Jennifer, but this was not helpful in the relationship between Mom and Grandma.

Jennifer who was Grandma's favourite over the years, hated Mom and wanted nothing to do with her due to difficulties throughout the years when she was growing up.

I experienced many problems with this young sister. If Jennifer did not agree with something, or if she believed lies about me, she called me names, using every foul word she could think of. I remember how she just stood and screamed at me.

I used to take care of her two boys and received nothing in return. For a period of time, I was with my nephews day and night; this was my thanks for helping her!

Dad had two that he got along with out of all of us: my younger brother, Ben, and my baby sister, Jennifer.

Occasionally Dad would mention within Mom's hearing, the woman he left behind in England. This happened especially when he was drunk. My youngest sister loved Dad and didn't care for Mom. Spitefully she went shopping one day and came home with a suitcase and a ticket for Dad to go to England to see the loved one he had left there.

Mom's heart was broken. How could her daughter do that to her? Dad decided not to go.

Through both their problems and their own dysfunctional lives they were ruining my life and those of my siblings. Things were miserable at home and I needed to get out before I lost my mind.

Fred was back in the house again. Dad, of course, had let him in. However, Fred stayed far away from me. Dad knew that I would have gone for help this time.

After Jennifer's marriage, she became a heavy drinker, and reacted poorly to a marriage that was falling apart. As a result she overdosed on drugs.

At this time my husband and I were living in an apartment down the hall from Jennifer and her husband. When we heard about Jennifer's predicament, we kept her awake and made her walk. This helped her to recover. Later in life she died of three aneurysms.

My younger brother Ben and I did not know each other well. He got along with Dad, and hated Mom since he was of the opinion that she was favouring Paul. He also became a mean, heavy drinker like Dad and was hardened by life as he grew up.

When I began having difficulty with my weight, I turned to the comfort of food as a crutch for the direction my life was taking. Ben called me names such as "big fat cow" or "pig." Perhaps he associated me with the pictures of a cow and a pig that Mom had on the fridge.

One day Ben and my sister, Susan, were chasing each other when Ben pushed her very hard into the car door. Half of her front tooth broke off. Ben thought it was funny and laughed at her. Dad and Mom also just stood there and laughed.

Ben married, had one child, divorced, and then remarried. Over the years I have seen him just a few times and we were polite with each other.

My brothers and sisters, as I discovered later, did not know what was happening to me, though some of them may have had their suspicions. I also became aware later that my sister, Susan, had similar experiences with Fred though with less frequency.

Susan, who has strength of will, told our parents to stop Fred or she would go for help. She also experienced frequent beatings but since she has always been capable of speaking out, she did not take a back seat to anyone.

One weekend when I was about fourteen years old, after Fred was allowed to return to our house, he came into the bedroom where the three of us girls were asleep. He approached the side of the bed where Susan was sleeping and started feeling her.

Susan yelled frantically and the household was awakened. Everyone came running. Susan screamed that Fred was in the closet, but Dad said that she was lying.

Mom had the courage to open the closet door, and there was Fred. All Dad said was that he better leave immediately.

Fred left the bedroom but not the house. The following day Dad and Fred were buddies as usual.

Though my feelings of hatred and mistrust continued, Fred seemed to take it seriously that he needed to stay away from me. By this time I was developing as a woman.

Mom and Dad beat Susan frequently. I heard the screams coming from her as she was tormented. Mom would hold her arms in an arm lock while Dad whipped her with his belt. Then Mom let go of her arms and Susan fell onto the floor. She crawled to the closet and stayed there for a while.

My aunt and uncle came for supper one day. Susan, who was five years old, got into mischief. My parents said that she was bad and Dad, who had been drinking, took Susan into the bedroom where he proceeded to beat her with his leather belt. I heard the screaming as she was hit.

My aunt, turning to Mom said, “What are you allowing? You could go to jail for this.”

Mom looked shocked, and my uncle who was Mom’s brother, told my aunt that it was none of their business.

Susan came out of the room sobbing, with welts covering her legs and backside. “Mom, Mom,” she cried. Yet she did not receive any comforting attention from her. There was no excuse for this.

When Susan was thirteen, she came home from school in a lot of pain. She could barely walk. Our babysitter called Mom at work and she had to come home. This made Mom very angry but she called the doctor who came to our house to examine Susan. He said that the problem was with her appendix and she needed to be taken to the hospital immediately where he would book her for surgery. The doctor also advised that she should be kept quiet.

Instead of calling Dad to take her to the hospital, Mom returned to work by taxi. The babysitter took care of Susan.

Dad got home in time for supper, followed by Mom's return from work. She then told Dad that Susan needed to go to the hospital because of the doctor's diagnosis of her appendix. Dad left with Susan about seven o'clock that cold winter evening. He first drove to the hotel, telling Susan that he was going in for a quick beer. She was left sitting in a cold car for two hours before being taken to the hospital.

The doctor, who was furious with Dad, quickly took Susan into the operating room for surgery. Her appendix had burst and she was full of poison. She was a patient in the hospital for two weeks.

My parents were firmly reprimanded by the doctors for their carelessness. My sister had almost died. Susan did not withhold the truth from the medical staff about what Mom and Dad did. They in turn became afraid that charges could be laid for child abuse.

Susan came home from that experience with a Christmas stocking full of candy and goodies. Mom took it away from her because she said the rest of us did not have any and she was going to have to share.

Some time after Susan came home from the hospital, just before Christmas, a big fight broke out between my parents. Mom threw over the Christmas tree.

My parents were uneasy and tense.

I do not know what became of the information about life at home that Susan had so freely shared, and my parents were not about to wait around to find out. We moved out of town soon after that.

Susan and I have established a closer relationship over the past few years.

Dad and Fred remained the best of friends. When Fred died, Dad and Mom attended his funeral. Mom did not want to go but Dad insisted that she be there with him. This man who had brought so much grief to my life had been caught molesting his sister's two boys. His sister and her husband told him that he had to stay away from them or he would go to jail. Now he was out of all our lives.

If I could have reacted at that time as I would today, Dad and Fred would have both gone to jail. Mom, as an accessory, would have had to submit to counselling.

Fear of my family caused me to move far from them, hoping to find some peace. That didn't help; my life just didn't get any better.

Chapter 2

Life with Jason

I met my first husband-to-be when I was fifteen and a half, during a time when I still enjoyed climbing trees. This occurred when my brothers met a friend at a Christian Youth Group where Jason attended. They were all going swimming and since the boys had forgotten their swim suits, Jason went along for the ride to get what they needed from home. He saw me sitting up in the tree. We started talking and eventually became friends.

In time we went out on a date along with Paul and Jason's sister, Veronica. We decided to go to the Theme Park just outside of town where we enjoyed each other's company while participating in enjoyable activities. On the way home, Paul took the wrong turn and we got lost. He quickly found a phone booth and called home to tell our parents what had happened. Curfew was at ten o'clock and we were an hour late.

Dad was very angry and Mom just stood there. He told Paul off and took the leather belt to me. "Why? How sick!" I thought as I stood there and submitted to the discipline. I had so much anger in me for both of them. They made my life a living hell.

After that, I stayed as far away from Dad as I possibly could. He would at times express himself by saying, "You're so much like your mother!" That showed me just how much he despised her as well.

Jason and I started seeing more of each other and began talking about marriage right after graduating from college. When Jason asked me to marry him, my younger sister overheard our conversation as she sat on the top step. She said: "Marry him because you won't get anyone else." In my mind I cared a lot for Jason. I loved him in the only way I knew, though I had not experienced affection and didn't know what love was. I was also desperate to get out of my home and away from my parents.

Mom and Jason's mother worked at the same hospital. They were both RNAs. They knew of each other and

admitted later that they did not like each other. Jason's mother called Mom and tried to stop the wedding.

Jason's family is super spiritual, mine is not. They thought that I was not good enough for their son. Jason, coming from a very large family, had his own issues. In addition, we were both so young.

The night before the wedding we were honoured at a large gathering of family and friends. At the conclusion, Jason and I decided to go to our new apartment to unpack some boxes in preparation for the move to our first home, following the honeymoon we had carefully planned together.

We were somewhat late getting back to the house though I realized that Dad still had me on a curfew. I had known that time was moving along and we needed to get back. I remained very afraid of Dad; he still had control.

When we returned he waited until Jason left and then turned on me with anger. "What do you think people are saying about you being late? Don't you care about your reputation?" he yelled at me.

Looking at him in shock, I thought to myself: "What are you talking about? I'm getting married tomorrow. Just one more day of this insanity and then I'll be out of this house!" This could have set a somber tone for the day ahead which was to be special.

Since my parents were paying for the wedding, I had to cooperate with them. "Fred," Dad said to me, "is going to drive the leading car. You and Jason will be in that car."

"NO," I responded, "he is NOT driving Jason and me."

However, Dad reminded me of who was paying for the wedding. "And he's driving!" Dad responded. I looked at him in disbelief and felt that I had no choice at this point but to go along with his plans.

The wedding was memorable and enjoyable in spite of most of Jason's family getting lost. Although I had noticed that Dad was having difficulty with my decision to get married, after we had waited for these family members to come, Dad eventually took my arm and said, "Too late!" I cried all the way to the altar. Jason's family arrived half way through the ceremony. What a way to start a marriage!

After the ceremony I observed the look on my mother-in-law's face. Her stern look was disheartening to me. It clearly indicated that she was not welcoming me into her family with open arms.

Before the reception, Jason and I, together with our entire wedding party, went to see my grandfather who was dying from cancer. He smiled at me, giving me a warm feeling of his approval. We then left to get our pictures taken.

The reception which followed was enjoyable for everyone. Later that evening Jason and I helped ourselves to leftover goodies and headed out-of-town for a weeklong honeymoon.

Since it had been a cold winter day that turned into a blizzard, we stopped at a lovely motel along the way. We spent the rest of the evening enjoying each other's company, and munching on the food we had brought, while watching TV.

It felt strange to undress in front of my new husband. Often I would do this in the dark. Yet the week was a lot of fun.

However, I missed my mother. I longed for her love as much at this time as I had throughout the years. I cried when I made a phone call to talk with her.

As I think back, I had so many problems in my life that I was dealing with from my experiences at home.

Feelings of devastation came over me.

When we returned from our honeymoon, we stopped at Jason's home. His mother looked angry as she stood in her kitchen. She wanted to talk with Jason about a gas bill for his use of the family car when he was going to college. As I was listening, she saw me and became very agitated. I was horrified when she gave Jason a hard slap across the face.

This was the super spiritual family I had married into! I was not good enough for their son, yet I became more aware of problems that his family had as well.

It was comforting to go to our first home which had one bedroom, a kitchen, living room, and bathroom. We were very comfortable there.

Again my dad showed his control over me. He found fault with our apartment which he thought was too expensive for the size.

We listened to him and moved into a smaller place that was somewhat cheaper. Now that one was a dump!

My parents tried to find everything wrong with Jason. In their eyes he could not do anything right. Both my family and Jason's were hurting our relationship as they continued to interfere in our marriage.

Jason's family was branded as being religious zealots and looked upon as self-centred by my family, my mother in particular.

My family was polite to Jason but it went no further until changes came when my husband turned twenty-one. They regarded Jason as one who was now of age, and able to start drinking. In my dad's eyes you were not a man if you did not drink.

All of my family frequently misused alcohol except my mother and me. Jason got more involved in this lifestyle because of the obvious influence they had on him. Fortunately, Jason did not become a heavy drinker like my father and brothers, but enjoyed it occasionally.

As a couple we raised a boy and a girl together. We had fun as a young family as we had many enjoyable times together. We loved our children very much and went together through good and bad times. They were number one in our lives.

I vividly recall the birth of our first child, our daughter, Amanda. I had been in labour for twenty-four hours when she was born with the umbilical cord around her neck. Our baby was blue and cold. The nursing staff put her into a warm incubator to get her temperature up to normal.

When our son was born, I was in labour for forty-eight hours. Nicholas was too big for me and I should have had a Caesarean section, the doctor told Jason. While in my pregnancy I had toxemia and a major infection. During the birth, I was torn quite badly because of his oversized head. I was in the hospital for two weeks and later developed an abscess the size of a grapefruit. It took a month to drain and a year for me to regain my strength.

With our parental responsibilities, Jason and I decided that I should stay home to raise the children while he worked. He also wanted to go and find a part time job to supplement his primary income.

My dad suggested that he get a job as a waiter in a hotel, serving food along with liquor. When he hesitated to get a job like this, my parents chided him and asked him if he thought he was too good to work in a hotel. My parents made my husband feel very insecure and unsure of himself. He yielded to their wishes, worked there for twenty hours each week, and found the pay to be very good.

There were repercussions. Since we were both Sunday school teachers in a strict evangelical church, Jason's hotel job was frowned upon.

It was Christmas season when the accident happened. One late night after work, Jason was driving home and crashed into a telephone pole. He sustained a concussion. The car was totalled. This was soon after the last payment had been made. We also did not have enough insurance to replace our small car.

Jason smelled of alcohol from the job he had just left. He was put into jail instead of the hospital. The police officer who was handling the case, was determined to lay charges against him. My brother-in-law's dad, a police officer, saw him with bruises in the cell, holding his head, but recognized him. He discerned Jason's need for medical care and arranged for him to be taken to the hospital. Since Jason had a reputation for controlling his alcohol consumption, this family friend was able to intervene.

Prayers for Jason were answered but there were further concerns. We had to find a car quickly for Jason to be able to get to work. Christmas was a meager event, we lost our positions in the Sunday School, and our reputation was tarnished. The minister, who was of great help to us, had served his term and consequently moved away. We were shunned. Our self-worth was gone.

We got into a habit of moving frequently throughout our marriage, sometimes every two years. I had a very difficult time staying settled and when negative things happened, we left and found another place to live. I felt a lot of turmoil inside of me. I was not experiencing peace.

I recall an incident one evening when Jason had not yet returned home from work. I had a habit of leaving the drapes open until late in the evening. This particular evening I walked into the living room to find a man peering in through the window. I screamed and he ran off. This gave me a lot of fear. Then we learned that there was a peeping Tom on the loose.

When Jason got home, I told him that we have to move. I was so afraid that this man would return. It worried me that there could be this danger when I was alone at night with the children. I imagined that he could break into our house. So we gave our notice and moved again.

Later when we had an opportunity to buy a house of our own, my dad had a serious talk with Jason and persuaded him to back out of the purchase. We always regretted that decision.

Dad continued trying to control our lives, putting us down for wasting money. Later I found out that he was embarrassed because he always rented his house and bought used cars. He spent his money elsewhere.

We were not allowed to celebrate our successes as a family. With every visit to my parents, our self-esteem was under attack and I was given neither love nor praise from them. Often they asked us why we came. I was craving approval from my parents but never got any.

With my family, Jason felt like a failure. In their minds there was never enough money.

However, Jason began to climb the ladder of success and worked longer hours. This resulted in him wanting to be at work more than at home. Eventually he became a work-a-holic, getting promotions, and gaining friends in the work place. Yet in the home we were having marriage problems.

When we needed our first loan, Dad suggested a finance company where he co-signed for us. This was a big mistake and it did not help our marriage. Dad still had control.

We got caught up in the game of yielding to allurements of increasingly higher loans as Jason stepped into better paying jobs. Every six or seven months the loan officer called us to say that we qualified for an extension on the loan until it finally caught up with us.

We did not understand that the loan company took our payments to cover the full amount of interest on a three year loan, and gave us a few hundred dollars as a bonus. We enjoyed spending the extra money, but this got us into making larger payments which took longer to pay off. Eventually we had to declare bankruptcy. For seven years we had a bad credit rating. This was certainly not a help to us.

It did not make any difference how much money we had after that. Our credit rating was worthless. In addition, we continued to move frequently.

During a time when we were still living near my parents, Jason and I met a couple who practiced partner exchange. The husband was infertile and they could not have their own children. Through a relationship with another man, his wife had become pregnant and had a child. They did not question this lifestyle. In fact, they wanted to have a second child.

This couple lived two doors down from us, and we got acquainted with them.

One cold winter evening, I went to visit Mom with our baby, Amanda. I was three months pregnant with our son, Nicholas, at the time. When I called home for Jason to get us, there was no answer.

Mom said: "He's probably over at your friend's place, sleeping with her." Mom was right. This neighbour lady had seduced Jason by giving him a strong drink and lured him into bed with her. She got pregnant with Jason's baby.

We did not know that it was his baby, though we were aware of her pregnancy. After the delivery, we went to visit and the father insisted that Jason hold the baby girl. I was not invited to hold her. As I think back, the baby did look like Amanda as an infant.

Eventually Jason told me what had happened. It was of no help in our marriage.

At a time when I was in my early twenties and the children were quite small, we became superintendents of apartment buildings.

The first building was small with twenty-four units. There we met a couple who, unknown to us, were having marriage problems. Jason became very friendly with this neighbour, Bruce, a pastor's son. The two of them went out drinking almost every night and Jason usually returned home drunk.

I drank only occasionally but not heavily.

I found out later that Bruce attempted to get Jason and me to exchange partners. One night Bruce came to our place where Jason started to drink with him. They offered me a drink and I had more than usual.

Jason got dopey and fell asleep. Bruce took advantage of the situation and came onto me. I was so drunk that I couldn't defend myself. He raped me.

When Jason awakened to realize what had happened he said, "Now we're even."

This comment was in reference to the time when he got my friend pregnant, and had a child with her. Jason was very apologetic about his comment as he knew it was wrong. He was dealing with the shame of what had happened in the past.

I went into deep depression. We went for counselling and were able to save our marriage at that time. Jason stopped drinking after this experience.

We made another move to an apartment building that belonged to the same company as the other two buildings we had supervised.

The third apartment that we lived in was in a high rise building which was approximately 30 years old. We were given one of the units for our use in exchange for our services in collecting rent, cleaning and maintaining the building.

After moving into the apartment we had to wait a few days for our phone to be hooked up. We were on the fourth floor and soon discovered that we were living next door to a drug addict.

We were new to the apartment, the job, and the area but trouble found us. Our neighbour hammered on the walls, cursing and acting crazy. He came banging on our door, threatening to kill us with a knife. We had no means of contact with anyone, without a phone, and Jason was unable to leave the apartment as we feared for our children who were six and seven years old. It was a very frightening time for us.

We prayed that someone would call the police, and during the early hours of the morning, the police arrived at our door which was identified as the superintendent's apartment. They came in response to a call someone had made. When we told them what was happening, they bodily removed the neighbour and charged him.

Another incident which occurred in that building involved Nicholas. One day he got on the elevator and encountered a tenant of the building who attempted to sexually assault him. We responded by following our pattern of running away and proceeded with another move.

Our next location, which lasted a year, was in an area with only a few houses which created a country-like setting. We lived on an estate with a wide-spread acreage. Many apple trees were in the back orchard. In the past, the house we occupied had been used for servant's quarters.

We had a living room, three bedrooms, a bathroom, a shed, and a basement, besides the new kitchen that had been built.

The former occupants of the house had been involved in witchcraft. We used to hear many strange noises in the house, especially when it was very quiet. We concluded that the place was haunted.

While living at this location we had a beautiful male husky dog, named Jessop George. One day while we were out shopping, a rabid fox came onto our yard. George was tied up on a long leash. The fox approached him and these two animals had a ferocious fight. George threw the fox and won the battle though he sustained wounds.

When we arrived home, the children petted George, and received his affectionate licks in return. It was not long before they noticed blood on our pet.

Jason and I noticed a trail of blood and wondered where it came from. We followed it and soon found a badly wounded fox lying in the brush. When we called the animal control centre, they sent someone to investigate and the fox was put out of its misery. Someone from the health department also arrived. The fox was taken away for testing and when the report was returned, it was confirmed that this animal had rabies.

George had to be checked out to make sure that he had obtained all the required needles. Then we built a fence around him and kept him in quarantine for weeks.

Since the children had been in contact with George and had sustained some of his blood on them, they were checked out by a doctor. It was a very worrisome time for us.

Since neither of them had open wounds, it was deemed unnecessary for them to be immunized.

Later we were told that there were problems with rabies where we were living. It was another traumatic situation that we had to get through. It all came to a good conclusion. The dog was well, as were the children. We thanked God for all the protection that He gave us.

At that time, because of what we saw happening in the evangelical churches, we decided to stop going to services where we had been participating in the activities. Their beliefs were very judgmental and you did as you were told.

This was not what God was telling us to do. God wants us to love one another. Christians need to realize that without love we are setting a poor example.

Yet, when we left that area, Jason and I decided to try an evangelical church again where we initiated a bus ministry. We visited in homes where many people lived with severe problems, where we saw abuse, drinking, drugs and violence. Other families without all these problems just wanted to be visited. Quite a number of these families began to go to the church.

Then some of the congregation complained to the pastor. They thought of the newcomers as destructive to the comfort of the church family. They did not want the disruption of those who brought problems, and it was upsetting to the church as a whole.

I always thought that the church was a place where people could be brought to learn about the Lord, to help one another, and for healing.

During this experience I was hoping to find a time when I could talk with Mom in private. I did not realize until later that whatever I said to her became known to other family members, but in her version. She seemed unable to speak truthfully about me.

Jason's family kept their distance from us as well. His mother continued to resent me and she influenced the rest of the family. I was able to communicate with one sister occasionally. The last year of his mother's life, she called me to apologize for helping to break up our marriage. I forgave her.

At this time our two children were getting close to their teen years, at eleven and twelve years of age. We believed it would be in our best interest to distance ourselves from family, so a decision was made to move hundreds of miles from our home area. In spite of having major marriage problems, my husband and I chose to move north. A couple we had met at a camp meeting invited us to move to the community where they lived. Through them our interest in native people developed. We wanted to do God's work and thought that by helping others, our minds would be distracted from our own difficulties. We had so much to learn.

This pleased my parents. I would no longer be a reminder to them of their past.

We got on a train and travelled for many hours to an isolated area, in a cultural setting different from what we knew, with a mixture of native and non native people. We were in shock when we got off the train at our destination to have the pastor tell us that we should just get back on the next train and return to where we came from. We stayed in spite of the obstacles.

There was no place to live and we started our adventures in this community by living in the back of a church. There were a few rooms we could stay in temporarily. It was very cold in this place and with little wonder. The kitchen wall had a large hole in it.

It was late fall and the river was not yet frozen over. The second evening we were there, we went for a walk by the dock. There we witnessed the discovery of a body that was being pulled from the water by the hair.

Some young fellows had been in a canoe on the river and because they were disoriented from drinking, their canoe capsized and one of them drowned.

What a beginning to this new chapter in our lives!

Our children had a difficult time making adjustments at the beginning of this relocation. We taught them that we are all God's children but the experiences Nicholas had at twelve years of age caused him to wonder.

Nicholas met a few boys who were friendly. As they were walking together, some of the local boys came up to him, sneering, "Whitey, go home." Then they pushed his head into a cement bridge.

At the same time, our thirteen year old daughter, who liked to wear some makeup, discovered this was definitely frowned upon, especially by the people in the church.

I felt sorry for my children as they experienced racial discrimination. It didn't take long to become aware that a lot of the native people resented having white people in their community. Amanda's peers in the church didn't want to associate with her.

Before the week ended we all wanted to go home.

As Amanda got involved with some girls from high school, it became evident that jealousy of any new comers created reprisal. At various times she was warned that they would slice up her pretty face. It helped a bit that by now we were beginning to know some people in the church.

Our temporary stay in the church for our accommodations came to an end and we moved into a shack with broken windows, a broken bunk bed, and no hydro. It was so cold, well below zero degrees. We wore our winter clothes to bed. In place of a toilet we used a slop pail. We had no phone for a long time.

We got a small wood stove and had to survive without hydro throughout the day. In the evening, the landlord sent an extension cord out so we had some lamp light until his family went to bed and he then shut off the power from us. We had to pay $350 a month to this family who attended the church. It was a nightmare.

One night when Jason and I were out, Amanda and Nicholas were with some young people in this shack. A fire started from the candle that was lit. Most of our clothes got burned.

Jason got a job and also did some work for the church.

Though I was kept busy moving numerous times, I also visited women in their homes. Many of these places were unbearably unsuitable. I found women who had been beaten by their husbands. Many of them bore black and blue marks from beatings as the result of heavy drinking.

One such woman was covered in blood and was drunk. It scared me.

I left quickly when I saw her husband returning. I walked out one door and her drunken husband came in the other door.

I was thirty-two at this time and looked very young for my age. I was in the habit of wearing jeans and was made aware of the gossip that was passed around that I was trying to look young, wearing clothes that made me look like a kid. A few of the women told me that if I did not change my style of clothing that they would kill me. It was unbelievable as I had always maintained a certain style. This put me on guard.

Amanda was having an increasingly difficult time because she got into the wrong crowd at school. Parents of the girls at church thought that she was too worldly. Amanda wanted only to have a friend.

Though some of the girls at school befriended her, they had their own ideas. In actuality, this group of girls was protecting Amanda from those who wanted to harm her because she was white and pretty.

One very cold winter day must have been about -50 degrees when Amanda had to go to the washroom. The slop pail was in the enclosed, but unheated back porch. We heard screams coming from the porch and found Amanda with her bum frozen to the pail. We had to use warm water to get her off. This is an incident we still talk about today and now find humorous.

My son, Nicholas, was frequently beaten up by other boys. He did not disclose much of what he experienced.

It became clear to me that it is not only white people who are prejudiced. I began to understand that this is true of all nationalities.

It soon became evident to us that in the area of this community where we were living, white people were regarded with contempt.

One Halloween day, Jason decided to wear a mask when walking home. A man yelled and cursed at him as he screamed, "White man, go home." He chased after Jason with an ax in his hand until he arrived home. We found that even walking on the streets posed danger for us.

This community had a small police station, a bigger store as well as a few small stores, a liquor store, a bank, two lodges, numerous churches, a clinic, and a few schools which included a high school and a college. A winter road, a small airport, a train station and gravel roads provided the means for transportation. The feeling of isolation could be overwhelming.

In one area there were some attractive homes but most of the houses in the community were in need of repair.

Legalism in the church continued to plague us. If we ever missed a meeting someone got after us and wanted to know why we were not in attendance. In their minds it indicated a backslidden state. They also frowned upon becoming friends with anyone from another church because they were regarded as sinners.

However, I became acquainted with some wonderful people from other churches. I have maintained those friendships to this day.

One friend who I will never forget was a white woman who married a native man. Her name was Linda and she moved to this community but suffered ridicule and was disowned by her wealthy family because she had married a native person. We were the best of friends until her death years later.

A couple from another church were a big help in keeping us sane. We are friends today and I thank God for them. Their children were also friends with Amanda and Nicholas.

When things became overwhelming I went to this friend's place. The structure of her home was one of the nicer places which reminded me of the kind I was used to from my years with my parents. It had the comforts of running water, and a bathroom with a toilet in it. However, unlike my experiences at home, I felt safe there.

I recall an incident when we were having lunch in the dining room of one of the lodges. It was a cold winter day on the weekend of a hockey tournament. There were a lot of people in town for this occasion.

Suddenly, two men who had been drinking were outside with their dogs and sleds, and began arguing. One of the men got out a hatchet to hit the other one. While some of the people in the lodge went outside to stop the commotion, I sat there in disbelief.

"We brought our children up here to this," I thought in anguish. "Oh my God, what a nightmare."

Dogs of all sizes ran freely throughout the town. Some of them created fear because when they ran in groups they were capable of attacking and injuring people.

A little black ugly dog sat outside one of the places where we lived. I adopted him as my little guard dog and named him Toby. He became my friend and comfort.

A man who was hired to catch stray dogs was aware of us befriending this dog. One day when we were not home, he came onto the property and took Toby, killed him and used his tail to earn more money.

We were all upset about the cruel action of this jerk but didn't get so much as a word of regret. He was using my dog's tail for profit.

I recall that over these years I still longed to become close to my mother. I called her daily. Sometimes she was civil with me but other times I was told that I was a bother to her. I wanted to visit her and when I showed up at her house she wondered what I was doing there and asked me what I wanted. Mom and Dad liked the idea that I was not living near them anymore. I felt total rejection. I was just a reminder of the past.

In my desperation to get recognition and love from my mother, I created a financial strain on my husband. The bills for placing those frequent long distance calls became large.

At a time when Mom was very ill and in the hospital, I travelled hundreds of miles to visit her. My nephew stood outside her room and asked me what I was doing there. I looked at him and said, "She is my mother. That's why I'm here." He then allowed me to go in and see her.

I couldn't believe it! What was my family saying about me? They did not want me around them. They made me look disgraceful to family and friends. How could my mother let Dad torment me? How could she tell such lies? I felt like completely turning my back on my family for what they did to me.

At another time we used a friend's phone to call my parents and let them know that we were planning a trip to visit them. We were looking forward to this change. Then just a few days before our scheduled departure, my parents called our neighbours to convey the message that they were too busy and that we were not to come.

The neighbours looked puzzled and wondered why they did not want us. I made up an excuse. It was a long time before I made any attempts to visit my parents again. I knew that they did not want us and there was nothing that I could do about it.

My parents made it very hard for me to forgive them. I was trying but the continuous actions against me made it so difficult. In time I did forgive them.

Although I was working for the church, I also got a job as matron at the police station. There were so many women with deep problems who were locked up in cells for drunkenness. I took care of the women who were put into the jail for intoxication and other problems.

One young woman who was very drunk was acting crazy. It was my responsibility to supervise her and to check on her every fifteen minutes. I repeatedly told the officers that she was very unstable but no one heard me. The last time I saw her before a horrible incident was when I returned to her cell and found her hanging from the bars. I screamed for help and for the keys. She had used her shirt to hang herself.

Officers came running and we removed her from this position. Then we tried to hold her down but she kicked and hit us. She did not know what she was doing. When I got in the way, she gave me a hard push and then kicked me. I left work with a concussion along with a sprained and bruised arm.

I recall an older lady who was brought into a cell by the police. The officers had difficulty controlling her.

She had created chaos at a party where she had beat up people and torn the place apart. She had demonstrated extra human strength.

The following morning this lady was as calm as a lamb. It was hard to believe that she had been so crazy the night before and had injured so many people.

I am firmly convinced that if you cannot drink socially, then totally stay away from alcohol because you become someone else.

Word was going around town that I was a turn coat because I was working with the police.

One evening, I was walking home with my son, Nicholas, when a group of older teens saw us and called: "There is the white bitch that works with the police. Get her!" I told Nicholas to run as fast as he could and not to look back.

We were chased all the way home but got in and locked the doors. I just could not believe all of this! My son was alright, though shaken up. We did not even have a phone to call for help.

Another day an older gentleman walked past me as I was on my way with a bag of groceries in my hands.

I greeted him with a smile on my face. He stopped, turned, and punched me in the stomach. Then I noticed that he was drunk.

One unforgettable event took place when Amanda visited one of her friends in another area of town. The temperature was forty below zero, and we did not know where she was. Her friend's family could not get their car started and did not have a telephone. So Amanda spent the night at her friend's home.

We had neither a car nor a phone, and with the possibility of frost bite, which occurs so quickly in severe cold, we had no way of trying to find our daughter. I spent a very fearful night as worries increased with each passing hour.

The next day, we got a ride to the high school. As I entered the office of the guidance counsellor, some of the students saw me and told Amanda. She was called to the office, and did not look happy when she saw me. This was the talk of the school for a while.

Amanda explained what had happened, and was told to go home after school. Though I was only trying to protect her, Amanda was not happy with me for a while.

Another time, Amanda was next door with some friends who were from a family connected to another church.

They were neighbours to Lucy and her girls. These girls repeatedly called Amanda names, and this time she reciprocated by calling them names. They reported this to their mother who was drunk and on drugs.

When the girls left that house to go to another friend's place, they were laughing and talking as they went. One of the girls looked behind her and saw Lucy, acting like a crazy woman, drunk and chasing after Amanda with a butcher knife.

Her friend screamed, "AMANDA, RUN, AND DON'T LOOK BEHIND YOU. YOU'RE BEING CHASED BY LUCY AND SHE HAS A KNIFE!"

Amanda got away. What saved her was God, and the woman unable to catch her because Amanda was a fast runner.

Jason and I did not hear about this immediately because Amanda went with her friends to another area of town and did not risk coming home until it was safe. Communication by phone was unavailable. When I found out, I went to the police. They said that there was nothing they could do until Amanda actually had been harmed.

Jason and I decided to send Amanda to his brother's family for her protection.

When Lucy learned that Amanda was sent out of town, she stated that if she could not get Amanda, she would go after her mother. I always had to watch my back after that. I could not even walk down town without getting into trouble.

It was hard to believe that people would act like this. They basically did whatever they wanted.

When we discovered that Amanda was spending most of her time alone in her room, and very unhappy at her uncle's place, we had to make other plans for her. She chose to live with my parents. I was not pleased about this arrangement but knew that they would be good to her. For almost a year she stayed there while attending hairdressing school.

My parents treated her well, because of course, she was not me. Amanda was unaware for the most part, at this time, of the horrible home life I had endured. When she completed her course in her late teens, she joined us again and wanted to start her own business.

After we came to the realization that it was time for us to leave this community, Nicholas and I went first. Jason stayed for a few more months before he joined us. .

When Jason left the north he found a good job. We moved twice while in this new area but our marriage was not holding together. We had a hard time even talking with each other though we had wanted to try and make things work.

Amanda found a place to start her hairdressing business with the help of her father. Jason always had a generous heart, and still does.

Nicholas was getting involved with the youth. He had a girlfriend, Rhoda, who was a polite young lady.

During the last few years of our marriage, intimacy had diminished until we lived like brother and sister. Our children finally had a talk with us and said that it was time for us to go our separate ways. We got a divorce but have remained the best of friends and included our new mates in this relationship.

It was difficult when my marriage ended. Jason and I had been in each other's lives since I was fifteen and a half years old, we have two children together, and we share many experiences of the past. Our determination to remain friends has been a choice that I will never regret.

Chapter 3

Life with Michael

It was in that far north native community which lacked the resources we were accustomed to, where I first met Michael. We all became friends and he got along well with my children.

Michael was eighteen and a half years younger than me. It was many years later that I developed a deep and sincere love for him, something I never imagined would happen. In my mind, the man should always be older than his wife, but I discovered that love does not regard age.

I was certain that we would encounter problems with Michael's family because I am white and divorced. Michael's mother was part white but she could never accept that. She taught her children that they were fully native. Most of them had problems with white people because they had formed negative ideas. Many of Michael's family viewed white people as their enemies, even though some of them took white spouses.

My family liked Michael even though they neither liked me, nor wanted me around. So it just did not matter. I was the one in love with Michael, and planned to marry him.

We decided to elope and have only a small group with us for this special occasion. We did not disclose our plans to Michael's family because they would have tried to stop us - and who knows what else.

Michael and I enjoyed a lovely little wedding and a reception that followed.

My husband's family had their own difficulties. Megan, my mother-in-law, often saw her first husband drunk and suffered from his abuse. He worked for a construction company and while on the job one day, he fell off the roof and died.

Megan then married his brother, Ralph, and had three more children. The oldest one died of pneumonia.

Ralph was very abusive with his family, and a heavy drinker. He would often beat Megan and the children. Megan also drank heavily. Life was extremely difficult for the children. They were all taken away at various times and placed in foster homes.

On one occasion, Ralph used an ax on Megan, cutting her across the face and head. He went crazy when he was drunk.

Ralph had a reputation for violence within the small community as well. When people saw him coming, they moved out of his way. He was able to go into the grocery or convenience stores and walk out with whatever he wanted. The store clerks were afraid that he would physically harm them if they tried to stop him. He found himself in trouble with the police often for drinking, theft, drugs, and assault for which he was repeatedly thrown into jail.

One day, Ralph could not find Megan. She had taken off with her sister, Joy. He discovered where they were hiding and he went there and kicked in the door. The women, who were waiting for him, beat him up with a large stick. Their plans had been to kill him but they changed their minds.

One day a preacher came to town and Michael's family went to the camp meeting where he was to be speaking. There they came under conviction for their violent lifestyle, accepted God's gift of salvation, and experienced drastic change in their lives. However, they went from one extreme to the other. They became self-righteous and extremely judgmental.

When Michael's family heard about our marriage, they were very angry. We did not know what to expect. When they finally came to see us, my mother-in-law told me that the only way she could love me was in the Lord. I sensed the insincerity as this comment was uncalled for. It only increased my feelings of uneasiness from her.

After they left, my husband said that we are better off staying away from his family. He knew what they were really like. Though he would have been able to see them whenever he wanted, he chose to interact with them only occasionally.

We kept our distance for a while, but heard the stories that were being spread about me, and why their son married me. Rumors went around that I had coerced Michael into marrying me, and that he felt he should marry me because I was pregnant.

The truth was that I was not pregnant when I married Michael. We were married because we loved each other. Such lies and stories! That is all I've known all my life.

We moved several times, making it hard to stay settled. It was also emotionally draining.

Michael and I talked about our family situation, and I tried to encourage him by saying that the Christian way is to get along with parents. He repeatedly said "No!" He told me that if we go back to any interaction with his parents and things go wrong, that he would not help me. I should have listened, but continued to wonder what would occur if something happened to them, and he had not spent more time with his parents. Would he blame me? It was still his mother in question here. Yet I carried the guilt of not listening to Michael.

I became pregnant with our little girl, Alexis. At the time of her birth, I had to undergo a Caesarean section because the placenta was in the wrong place. I was told that both the baby and I could have hemorrhaged to death, but thankfully we both survived very well. The baby resembled both of us and was beautiful. At birth the baby was brown skinned, but as the year went by she became light coloured. It would not have mattered to us either way.

Michael phoned his parents to relay the news and invited them to come and see the baby. At their arrival, they brought some other family members with them.

Michael, who was unsure of how to handle this situation, was very aware of how these guests entered our home by ignoring me and actually giving me dirty looks. I was so relieved that my son, who had come to live with us briefly, chose to stay in the house for a while during this tense occasion. He waited until later to go out to what he had planned to do that evening.

Michael showed off the baby and while his mother was holding her, she commented, "The baby looks just like one of us." Then she turned to her husband and said, "You can hold the baby too because she looks like one of us!"

I quickly yelled out from the kitchen, "She is also like her mother!" Everyone became quiet and these visitors left shortly after.

Occasionally Michael's parents came to see us. Each time they stepped inside the door, my father-in-law remarked, "There's just Indians in here, no white man."

My response was always, "There's both." I realized that it was his attempt to irritate me.

My mother-in-law sometimes had talks with me saying, "Someday I'll get all my boys back." I would just look at her and say, "Really!"

One day the two of us were having coffee together in a restaurant when one of her friends approached her and I was introduced to her. Her friend said, "Is this is the one you've been talking about to us?" I just looked at my mother-in-law but she did not say a word in front of me to her friend.

I recall the day when Michael's brother, Eric, came to visit us. While Michael went to the back room to change his clothes, I made a lunch for Eric. As he was eating, I folded laundry and chatted with him. We were having a meaningful conversation when he suddenly blurted out, "The reason I came here today was to kill you."

"What?" I responded in complete shock.

He repeated his intent, "Yes, I came here to kill you!"

I asked him, "Why?" He said that his mother hated me and didn't want me in his brother's life, as well as that of her granddaughter.

I became very frightened, and Eric said that he had changed his mind because he found me to be a nice person.

We saw Eric only occasionally over the years until he died of a drug overdose. He had lived a rough life, and spent time in jail for arson, drugs, drinking and assault charges.

Most of the family had drinking and drug addictions.

Michael's oldest brother was the most accepting of their family. He became an assistant pastor. His wife, Fran, who was older than her husband by ten years, had also been with another man and had a child. There were these similarities between Fran and myself, yet the parents accepted her because she was native. Fran was kind to everyone. Sadly, she died of cancer about a year ago.

I dared to begin a friendship with one of my mother-in-law's sisters. We interacted by phone but she told me that I could not say anything to Michael's mother because she didn't like me. She had to stay loyal to her sister. I then decided not to bother anymore, and spoke with her only briefly if we happened to meet each other.

When the parents or one of Michael's siblings and their partners came to see us, I was never left alone in the room with one of the boys. Their mom had told them that I was not to be trusted.

There were so many problems with Michael's family. We were victims of hurts and untrue stories. When I talked to Michael about the lies which were being spread about us, he reminded me that he had wanted to stay away from his family. Now he firmly insisted that he was going to stay out of it.

Michael was a wonderful man but he could not deal with stress. On his days off from work he occupied himself with drawing and building. He was a very capable artist, and enjoyed working with his hands, building with wood.

We attempted to get involved in a church until we began to notice how cruel church members could be. The petty competitions to outdo each other, the gossip, the man-made rituals, the judgment passed if anyone should slip, and the hypocrisy were very disheartening. Where love and kindness should have resided, there was a rod of punishment which poisoned the sacred environment. Eventually we realized what was happening and disassociated ourselves by leaving. We continued to practice our faith at home but no longer went to church.

Michael was brave enough to try some other churches. If he did not agree with what was taught, he would be asked to leave.

One time when we had just moved to a town following Alexis' birth, we were trying to get settled and Michael was looking for work. He called a few churches for some help but they turned him down. He actually went to one church but they said, "NO" because he was not attending there. They helped only their own.

Most of us Christians take care of only our own and thereby set a bad example for others.

During the time of one visit when Michael's parents and some other family members were at our house, Alexis was playing near the dining room table. Her grandma turned to her sister and called Alexis a half breed. Then she laughed at her own remark. I found this very rude and insulting, and again realized this is the way they talked about people of different colour. Though it is not right, having said this in front of her granddaughter made it even more disrespectful.

For the first years of our marriage, Michael drank very little. That changed in later years, before his mother's death. He, like me, wanted his mother's love but didn't receive it.

Michael had become friends with my ex-husband, Jason. When Jason's second marriage failed, he left where he had been living and moved nearer to us. The two girls from his second marriage stayed with their mother while Jason got visiting privileges. Everyone got along this way.

Michael's parents had not appreciated that we were all on friendly terms. They thought there was something wrong with that. In their way of thinking, it would have been better if we all hated one another through which the children would have suffered. I believe many individuals are of this opinion.

Later, when Jason needed a place to stay, Michael asked him to board with us. It was originally intended to be for a short while, but he stayed for seven years. Jason had his own living space and we all got along. During this time, Jason and Michael developed an even closer friendship.

Jason became godfather to Alexis. We did not care how weird this seemed to some people. We thrived on the cooperation and contacts with all the children.

When Michael became very ill from a huge stomach ulcer, he almost died when it perforated. He was in the hospital for two weeks and off work for twelve weeks. A nurse came twice daily to care for the two infections in his stitches, and to change and dress the wound. His health never returned to what it had been. He was later readmitted to the hospital when he hemorrhaged from his bowel.

Up until this time we had been renting accommodations, but desired a house of our own. We began to look for a suitable house and location. One day Michael, Alexis and I went house hunting and found one that we were interested in purchasing.

We needed some help with the down payment and since Michael's parents had inherited some money, he approached them about giving us a loan. We planned to repay this money in a short while with interest.

Again, Michael faced disappointment. His parents refused to help us, though we knew that they had done so for other family members. I was convinced that their response was because they did not like me, and they took it out on him.

I noticed my dear husband beginning to change after that.

Michael started to drink more, and when he got drunk, he remembered the past which he had attempted to bury. At times he became verbally mean; he also sat and cried about his past and his failures. He talked repeatedly about his step father, who was also his uncle. He recalled the beatings this man gave his mother and his attempts to kill her with an ax or other objects. Michael never hit me but hurt himself by banging the wall with his fist. He threw objects and took a hammer to his hand. He wanted to die.

I like to remember Michael's true nature. He had a heart of gold and would do anything for anyone. He had a very kind and loving personality.

When one of Jason's daughters and future son-in-law were looking for a temporary place to live, Michael said they could live with us. I wish this would never have happened. They stayed for a year and it was hell. She said and did everything her fiancé told her to, and his attitude was appalling. With his aggressive personality he was cruel to everyone. He constantly complained about everything from the cooking to the volume of the TV. We all walked on eggshells because of him. Though Michael had allowed them to stay because of Jason, we finally had to tell them to get out. Jason was regretful over the way this had worked out.

Meanwhile, Jason met a wonderful lady, moved in with her, and later married her. We enjoyed her friendship as well until she died of cancer. It was a very sad time for all of us.

My son Nicholas got married to Ann, a lovely person, and Michael was his best man. It was a huge, beautiful wedding on a warm summer day.

When Nicholas and his attractive bride went on their honeymoon, unknown to the couple, one of Ann's aunts decided to play a joke on them. She fastened a sign on the back of the car they used: Help me. I'm being kidnapped.

Along the way to where they intended to go, they stopped at a gas station to fill up the car. The gas attendant saw the sign, wrote down the license plate numbers and called the police.

Two police cruisers appeared and stopped the car. One of the officers told Nicholas to get out and put up his hands. When they were questioned about the sign, Nicholas and Ann admitted that they were unaware of it but that it must be a prank.

The police officers did not find it amusing. In fact they were very cross.

Upon hearing about this, we were quite upset to think that someone would play a joke like this. It could have caused a major tragedy.

Later my oldest daughter, Amanda, got married. Though this relationship ended in a divorce, she speaks with her ex-husband if she sees him.

When Michael's mother got very sick, Michael, Alexis and I drove to the hospital to see her. I vividly recall that my father-in-law shunned me.

With everyone together, a family picture was taken. We all stood in line. One of Michael's cousins was behind me, put her hands on my back and pushed me. I fell out of line but went back to where I had been standing.

That evening, the sister who had befriended me, gave me dirty looks, shunned me, and refused to talk to me.

The following morning I was in the waiting room with family members. Michael rushed in to get me, saying, "She's going. Come now."

I was full of fear. My husband fell apart and I could not help him because he did not want it. I hid in a public washroom for a while and Alexis stayed with her dad. Then I snuck out and hid behind our car until Michael and Alexis came out. I did not feel safe and did not attend the funeral.

After the loss of his mother, Michael went through a very difficult time. He wanted and needed her love so much and never received what he craved. Now he drank even more heavily and became verbally more cruel and cutting. His mood swings became more noticeable.

Our daughter, Alexis, was listening to all of this. It was so hard on her, especially when I bore the brunt of her father's anger.

A few years later, Michael's step father died from a heart attack.

I remember my mom's call one day. She asked if Paul could stay with us for a while. Dad did not want him around as they were not getting along. We agreed to have him live with us for a while.

Paul's drinking was out of control. On one cold winter evening he decided to go to the bar. He had a short distance to walk, just through the back yard and down the street.

We left the door unlocked until we went to bed at twelve-thirty. We didn't know when Paul would return home. At any rate we had given him a key.

After we had been in bed for a while, my husband heard someone knocking at the back door. It was Paul with frozen hands, swollen and blue from the bitterly cold night. He was so drunk that he was unable to see straight.

We wanted to take him to the hospital but he refused, and we didn't want to force him against his wishes. Instead we put his hands under cold water and rubbed them to improve the circulation. His hands were never the same again.

A friend of the family went to the bar the following day to find out what had happened. The owner said that Paul had been so drunk that he started a fist fight with another patron. Paul was thrown out and told to never return.

Paul recalled the next morning that he had passed out in the back yard and when he came to his senses, he had forgotten that he had the key to get into the house. When he returned to my parent's home he told everyone that we had locked him out.

My brother had to create a story so that Dad would let him return home.

We were blamed for the condition of his hands. The story spread that they were damaged because of us.

Just another set of lies! Was it ever going to stop?

When my father was dying, Michael and I travelled to see him and to be of help to Mom. When we got back to my parent's apartment from the hospital, he told me that he could not believe what my mother had said about me. He caught her in a lie! I did not want to believe it; this was so embarrassing to me. My mother could not separate the lies from the truth.

Michael and I had a deep love for each other but we had our own individual issues to deal with. I wish that I could turn back the hands of time and change things but that cannot happen.

The night before Michael died, he drank heavily. He could not control himself with his mouth and said some vicious and cruel things to me. Then his emotions changed and he cried uncontrollably, hysterically screaming that he wanted to die. Later he came out of the bedroom and wanted me to come to bed. I could not move, but just sat and felt very confused and alarmed.

The next morning at 5 AM, I went to the room to wake him up and then left to place a phone call, asking for prayer. I did not know what else to do. Then when I returned to the room Michael had already left for work.

He took his bicycle instead of the car that day. As he proceeded down the little hill outside of our house, he had a massive heart attack and lost control of his bicycle. He went through at a stop sign and rammed into a car window.

I knew something had happened to him when I heard the sirens from police cars and an ambulance. I screamed for my oldest daughter who was staying with us at that time. She ran down the street to see what had happened.

I was certain in my heart that it concerned Michael. A police officer came back to the house with my daughter and told me that my husband was still alive. Since I could not drive, Amanda quickly drove me to the hospital. Alexis stayed at the house for the police to return. When the officer did not come back, Jason hurriedly picked her up and brought her to be with us at the hospital.

Meanwhile, Amanda and I were taken to the trauma room where I was told that Michael had very little chance of living.

The police told me later that they had found a half full bottle of whiskey in Michael's backpack.

When Michael saw me, he tried to sit up and pull up his mask. He looked directly into my eyes, told me that he loved me, and then stopped breathing. He was brought back twice and then put into an induced coma.

I remained at his bedside except for a few breaks and an attempt to get a few hours of rest.

The following day, with Alexis, Amanda, and me around his bed, Michael passed from this life into the next. His emotional suffering was over. I was able to get through the next few days because I knew that Michael was now in a better place.

When we went home from the hospital, I had to decide if I was going to let his family know that he had died. Part of me was so angry that I wanted to wait until after the funeral. However, for the sake of my husband, I chose to call them.

I recalled how Michael used to phone them and they hardly ever returned his calls. I always felt that it was because of me, because they listened to whatever their mother had told them.

I made a call to Michael's oldest brother and of course he didn't answer the phone. So I left him a message and yelled it into the phone: "YOUR BROTHER JUST DIED! HOW ABOUT RETURNING THE

PHONE CALL IF YOU WANT TO KNOW WHAT HAPPENED!"

He returned my call immediately and I was not very nice to him. It all came out: "You could hardly ever return any of Michael's phone calls. He just wanted to be loved by his family, and all of you hardly bothered with him because your mother didn't accept me."

"Furthermore," I stated with firmness, "You can all come to the funeral. This will be Michael's day, but tell everyone that if any problems are created, I will call the police to have that person thrown out. DO YOU UNDERSTAND ME?"

I was determined to make the day of the funeral special for my husband and no one was going to ruin it because of their dislike for me.

I was not home long from the hospital before I got a call from the attending doctor who wanted permission to do an autopsy. When I denied his request he asked me why not as they would cover up the stitches.

I told him that they had explained to me why Michael died. They gave him many tests, x-rays and an MRI. Sarcastically, I said: "In other words you're saying that he didn't die from what you said? You treated him for the wrong thing?!"

"Why don't you want him to have an autopsy?" countered the doctor.

"We don't believe in our loved ones being cut up. You are all butchers! I give you permission for nothing!" I cried.

Then the doctor asked to speak to my son or daughter. My daughter took the phone and gave him the same answer that I had.

He then identified himself as the assistant coroner, and said that he would call right back. When he did, he said that they had enough information and an autopsy was not necessary.

Next the request came to take Michael's heart and study it since there was a known family history of heart problems. I denied them again.

"All right, goodbye. His body is ready to go." I was told.

One more call came from the hospital with a request to take some tissue from my husband's body. I screamed, "NO!! What is his body still doing there? Don't call again!" She said, "Goodbye" and hung up the phone.

A lasting impression gives me the idea that many of these professionals are heartless and cold.

In preparation for the funeral, I talked with the pastor who was taking the service. I told him about Michael's family and what he could possibly expect because of their dislike for me.

The funeral was large with many people coming to share in the grief.

I was relieved that it went well and Michael had a good send-off. Everything had been planned for Michael's sake, not my own. I had asked three of his brothers to be pall bearers, as well as my son and some friends of the family. Michael's older brother and my son gave the eulogy.

The atmosphere of the room at the funeral luncheon seemed cold and empty to me. Michael's family stayed completely away from the rest of us.

Alexis and I do not hear much from any of Michael's family anymore.

Michael and I have been so blessed with a beautiful daughter who makes us proud. I brought baggage from my past into our marriage, and he did likewise. Yet we loved each other and always will.

My dear husband is so missed. I told him before he died that we wanted to make him proud, always.

Chapter 4

Conclusion

I am still sitting here, dear reader, on my window ledge as the snow falls outside, having remembered such vivid details of my past.

My central thoughts return to the loss of my dear husband. I miss him immeasurably. We went through so much together; now he is gone from sight.

Flashbacks of my life as I was growing up, which included endless pain, anguish and devastation, leave me drained of energy. Memories of various family members and friends gone through death have only increased the depressing mood within me. My mind adds to that, my two marriages, my children and friends, the church community, multiple moves, financial difficulties, and so much more.

I am thankful for my three grandsons: Tommy, Roger and Austin. They are great boys.

I realize now that I have been overprotective of my two girls. To this day I struggle with fear of what could happen to them. It is neither healthy for them nor for me. My younger daughter is now 25 years of age, and it is time to let go.

No matter what we are going through, we have to remember that we are not alone. There is help available through counsellors, staying focused, and refusing to keep it all bottled up before those suppressed feelings come out in a way that bring harm to you or someone else. Start thinking positively about yourself and stay strong so you can rise above all things. Keep in mind that it takes time.

I also learned about forgiveness. It frees the mind from devastation and the darkness that often becomes overwhelming.

Both of my husbands had complained about me leaving lights on at night. They recognized the increased cost on our hydro bills, but I could not sleep in the dark. Today as I make greater attempts to limit the light to only one, I still feel like I am suffocating and get overwhelmed in the dark.

There are still things that I need to work through. I do not know what the future holds for me, but I move ahead one day at a time.

I keep in mind that I am a survivor, not a victim.

Any comments or questions about this book can be sent to: iwasachildbutnot@hotmail.com

Printed in the United States
By Bookmasters